Homes of living things

Bobbie Kalman

Crabtree Publishing Company

www.crabtreebooks.com

Created by Bobbie Kalman

Dedicated by Crystal Sikkens
To my wonderful husband Jonathan,
for all the time you've spent making our house a home.

**Author and
Editor-in-Chief**
Bobbie Kalman

Editors
Reagan Miller
Robin Johnson

Photo research
Crystal Sikkens

Design
Bobbie Kalman
Katherine Kantor
Samantha Crabtree (cover)

Production coordinator
Katherine Kantor

Illustrations
Barbara Bedell: page 24 (den, desert, forest, and grassland)
Halina Below-Spada: page 24 (habitat)
Jeannette McNaughton-Julich: pages 19, 21, 24 (burrow and lodge)
Trevor Morgan: page 24 (hive)
Bonna Rouse: pages 23, 24 (cave)
Margaret Amy Salter: page 24 (nest and tree)
Tiffany Wybouw: page 22

Photographs
© BigStockPhoto.com: page 13 (bottom)
© Dreamstime.com: page 5 (bottom right)
© iStockphoto.com: front cover, pages 5 (bottom left), 10 (bottom)
© 2008 Jupiterimages Corporation: pages 12, 13 (top), 14 (right), 16,
    17 (bottom left), 20 (top)
© ShutterStock.com: pages 1, 3, 4, 5 (top left and right), 6, 7 (left), 8, 9 (bottom),
    10 (top), 11, 14 (left), 17 (all except bottom left), 18, 19, 20 (bottom), 22, 23
Other images by Corel and Digital Vision

Library and Archives Canada Cataloguing in Publication

Kalman, Bobbie, 1947-
    Homes of living things / Bobbie Kalman.

(Introducing living things)
Includes index.
ISBN 978-0-7787-3228-0 (bound).--ISBN 978-0-7787-3252-5 (pbk.)

    1. Animals--Habitations--Juvenile literature. I. Title.
II. Series.

QL756.K35 2007   j591.56'4   C2007-904244-9

Library of Congress Cataloging-in-Publication Data

Kalman, Bobbie.
    Homes of living things / Bobbie Kalman.
        p. cm. -- (Introducing living things)
    Includes index.
    ISBN-13: 978-0-7787-3228-0 (rlb)
    ISBN-10: 0-7787-3228-2 (rlb)
    ISBN-13: 978-0-7787-3252-5 (pb)
    ISBN-10: 0-7787-3252-5 (pb)
    1. Animals--Habitations--Juvenile literature. I. Title. II. Series.

QL756.K355 2007
591.56'4--dc22

2007027221

Crabtree Publishing Company

www.crabtreebooks.com   1-800-387-7650

**Published in Canada
Crabtree Publishing**
616 Welland Ave.
St. Catharines, Ontario
L2M 5V6

**Published in the United States
Crabtree Publishing**
PMB16A
350 Fifth Ave., Suite 3308
New York, NY 10118

**Published in the United Kingdom
Crabtree Publishing**
White Cross Mills
High Town, Lancaster
LA1 4XS

**Published in Australia
Crabtree Publishing**
386 Mt. Alexander Rd.
Ascot Vale (Melbourne)
VIC 3032

Contents

What is a home?   4

Habitats and homes   6

Hiding places   8

Cave shelters   10

Dens in holes   12

High up in trees   14

All kinds of nests   16

Under the ground   18

A beaver lodge   20

Insect homes   22

Words to know and Index   24

What is a home?

Living things are people, animals, and plants. People and animals need places to live. They need places to sleep and feel safe. They need **shelter** from the weather. Shelter protects living things from rain, snow, sun, and wind. People and animals live in many kinds of homes.

Some homes are small and have only one room. This home is far from towns or cities.

Some homes are in tall apartment buildings that are in cities.

Some homes have many rooms and big yards. This family lives in a large home.

Animals live in different homes, too. This home is under ground.

Habitats and homes

Habitats are the natural places where plants grow and where animals live. Plants grow in habitats, but they do not live in homes. Animals live in habitats, and some also live in homes. Some habitats have a lot of rain. Some habitats are hot and dry. This habitat is a **grassland**. What kind of plants are growing here?

Forests are habitats with many trees and other kinds of plants. Forests grow in hot and cold places. This forest is a **rain forest**. Rain forests get a lot of rain.

Many animals live in rain forests. This monkey lives in a hot rain forest.

Deserts are dry habitats. There is very little rain in deserts. Cactuses are plants that grow in some deserts. Cactuses do not need a lot of water. This owl lives on a cactus.

7

Hiding places

Animals live in habitats, but not all animals have homes. Animals that do not have homes in their habitats find safe places to hide from other animals. This baby deer is lying on the ground in a forest. It is hidden by the forest plants around it.

There are hiding places in water, too. This tiny fish is hiding in a hole in the ocean. The frog below lives in a pond habitat. It hides among some water plants that grow there.

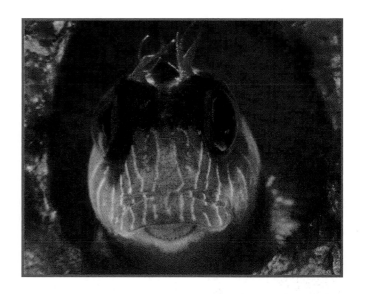

Cave shelters

A **cave** is a hole in the side of a hill or under the ground. It can be small or huge. Why is a cave a good shelter for this wolf and this bear?

This rattlesnake lives in a desert. Its home is a cave. The cave protects the snake from the hot sun. There are caves under water, too. These fish are hiding in a cave. They see a shark!

Dens in holes

Some animals are **predators**. Predators hunt and eat other animals. Predators look for young animals to eat because young animals are weak. They cannot fight back. Most animal mothers hide their babies so predators will not find them.

These arctic fox babies are hiding in a hole in the ground.

Mothers hide their babies in **dens**. A den is a home inside an opening. A cave is a den. A hole in a log can be a den, too. This bobcat kitten lives in a tree trunk.

This raccoon family's den is in a hollow log. Do you think this den is a safe home?

High up in trees

This woodpecker is bringing food to its babies inside a tree hole.

Many animals live high up in trees. Woodpeckers make holes in trees for their babies. This barn owl has found a hole in a tree for her babies. Raccoons and squirrels also live in trees.

Are these raccoons safer high up in a tree or on the ground? Why?

Chimpanzees live in hot, rainy, forest habitats.
At night, chimpanzee mothers and their babies
sleep high up in trees. Many predators cannot
climb, so the babies are safe there. Chimpanzee
mothers use leaves to make their beds soft.

All kinds of nests

Some animals find homes in their habitats, and others make homes. Many birds build nests in which to lay their eggs. The **chicks**, or baby birds, **hatch** in the nests. To hatch is to break out of an egg. The chicks are safe in their nests.

This wood pigeon has built a nest of twigs for its babies.

Gentoo penguins live in very cold habitats. Few plants grow there. Gentoo penguins make nests from stones and anything they can find. How do you think the nests feel?

This bird has made
a nest on water.

This squirrel lives in
a nest high up in a tree.

Under the ground

Many animals live in **burrows**. Burrows are tunnels that animals dig in the ground. Some animals live in burrows to keep their babies safe. Some animals live in burrows to keep cool. Other animals live in burrows to keep warm. Two little groundhogs are peeking out of their burrow.

Prairie dogs live in grasslands called **prairies**. Prairie dogs dig long burrows, called **towns**, under the ground. There are tunnels and rooms in each town. Many prairie dogs live in one burrow. The burrows are cool in summer and warm in winter. Explain why you think these burrows are safe places.

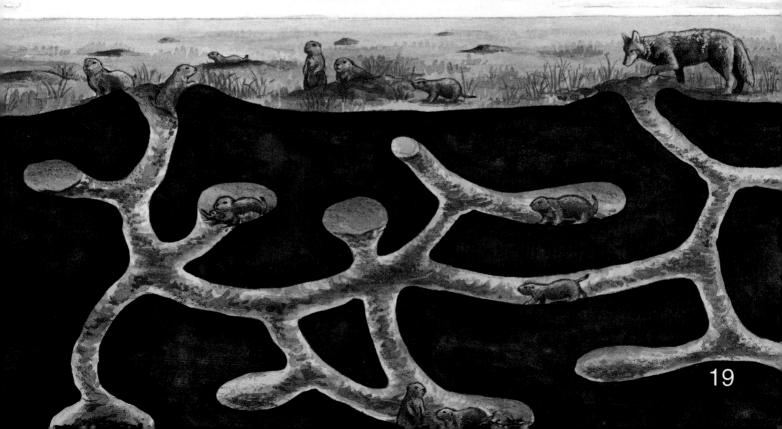

A beaver lodge

Beavers build homes in water. The homes are called **lodges**. Beavers build lodges in deep water in rivers or lakes. Lodges are safe from predators because it is hard to get into them.

Beaver lodges are made of branches and mud. There is a hole at the top for air.

Beavers have sharp teeth. They use their teeth to cut down trees. Beavers use tree branches to make their lodges. There is only one way to get into a lodge. It is under water. There is an extra tunnel for escape in case a predator gets into the lodge. Do you think a beaver lodge is a safe animal home? Explain why or why not.

Insect homes

Many kinds of insects make homes. Wasps make **hives**. A hive is a nest. Many wasps work together to make a hive. Insects that live together in big groups are called **colonies**. This wasp colony is making a hive.

22

Bees make hives, too. Each part of a hive is called a **cell**. Every cell has six sides. What is this shape called? It is a **hexagon**! Some cells have young bees inside. Some have honey. How do you enjoy honey? Do you eat it on toast?

Words to know and Index

prairie dog

burrows
pages 18-19

caves
pages 10-11, 13

dens
pages 12, 13

deserts
pages 7, 11

forests
pages 7, 8, 15

grasslands
pages 6, 19

habitats
pages 6, 7, 8, 9,
15, 16, 17

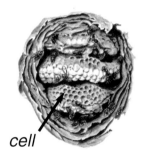
cell

hives
pages 22-23

beaver

lodges
pages 20-21

nests
pages
16-17, 22

trees
pages 7, 13,
14-15, 17, 21

Other index words

colonies page 22
people page 4
predators pages 12,
  15, 20, 21
shelter pages 4, 10
rain forests page 7

24

Printed in the U.S.A.